Advice from Dead Celebrities

A. J. Barnes

Illustrated by
Aaron Waite

Aadamsmedia

Avon, Massachusetts

Published by
Adams Media, a division of F+W Media, Inc.
57 Littlefield Street, Avon, MA 02322. U.S.A.
www.adamsmedia.com

ISBN 10: 1-4405-3002-5
ISBN 13: 978-1-4405-3002-9
eISBN 10: 1-4405-3058-0
eISBN 13: 978-1-4405-3058-6

Printed in the United States of America.

10   9   8   7   6   5   4   3   2   1

Library of Congress Cataloging-in-Publication Data
is available from the publisher.

*This book is available at quantity discounts for bulk purchases.
For information, please call 1-800-289-0963.*

Advice from Alive Lawyers

The pearls of wisdom on the following pages have not been provided or endorsed by any of the celebrities whose names appear in this book—though that should be blindingly obvious given that they all have one thing in common: every last one of the people mentioned in this book is dead.

Sadly, the deceased have played no part in contributing to this book. Perhaps even sadder, the advice enclosed is exclusively the diseased imagining of the Author, and even he refuses to be held accountable for damages caused by anyone dumb enough to take anything in this book seriously.

So while we invite you to sit back and chuckle/gasp in horror/ read aloud to similarly sick-minded individuals, we do have one very real piece of advice for you:

Do not try this at home.

Dead Offering Advice

Mama Cass Elliot

AMERICAN SINGER, MEMBER OF THE MAMAS & THE PAPAS
(September 19, 1941–July 29, 1974)

Chew your food
thoroughly and carefully.

Julia Child

AMERICAN CHEF, AUTHOR, TELEVISION PERSONALITY
(August 15, 1912–August 13, 2004)

One day, all that butter will catch up to you (I'm looking at you, Paula Deen).

Don Knotts

AMERICAN COMIC, ACTOR
(July 21, 1924–February 24, 2006)

Playing second fiddle will only leave you whistling "Dixie."

John Lennon

BRITISH MUSICIAN, SONGWRITER
(October 9, 1940–December 8, 1980)

Bros before hoes.

Corey Haim
Get lost.

Brandon Lee
Don't bring a gun to a fake fight.

Andrew Koenig
Every boner has a tragic ending.

Amy Winehouse

If they try to make you go to rehab,
say, "Yes, yes, yes."

Karen Carpenter

Breakfast is the most important meal of the day.

Christopher Marlowe

Avoid bar brawls and keep your ideas to yourself.

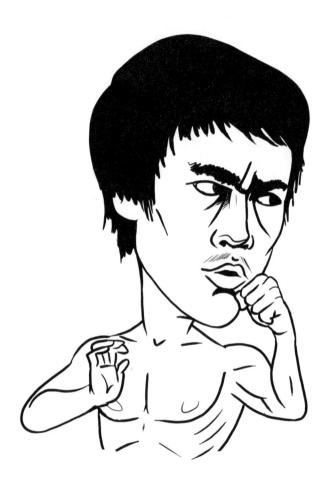

Bruce Lee

CHINESE-AMERICAN ACTOR, MARTIAL ARTIST
(November 27, 1940–July 20, 1973)

The family that works together, dies together.

Gary Coleman

AMERICAN ACTOR
(February 8, 1968–May 28, 2010)

Being a child star
is a tall order.

Marlon Brando

AMERICAN ACTOR
(April 3, 1924–July 1, 2004)

Here's an offer you can't refuse—a little diet and exercise never killed anyone.

John Ritter

AMERICAN ACTOR, VOICEOVER ARTIST, COMEDIAN
(September 17, 1948–September 11, 2003)

It's only cool to have a
dumb blonde for a room-
mate if she's dumb enough
to sleep with you.

Vincent van Gogh

I said, DON'T listen to a word people say. Let it go
in one ear and out the other.

Charles M. Schulz

When life hands you rocks, bitch to the lesbian.

Evel Knievel

White men *can* jump.

Curly Howard
Stupid sells.

Desi Arnaz
Always be prepared to 'splain yourself.

Charlton Heston
When I said, " . . . from my cold, dead hands,"
I was joking. Well, I guess you have my guns now.

James Dean

AMERICAN ACTOR, CULTURAL ICON
(February 8, 1931–September 30, 1955)

Click it or ticket.

Bela Lugosi

HUNGARIAN STAGE AND SCREEN ACTOR
(October 20, 1882–August 16, 1956)

Typecasting really sucks the fun out of things.

John Candy

CANADIAN ACTOR, COMEDIAN
(October 31, 1950–March 4, 1994)

Canadian bacon + morbid obesity = fatal heart attack.

Burgess Meredith

AMERICAN ACTOR

(November 16, 1907–September 9, 1997)

Eat lightning and
crap thunder.

Pat Morita

AMERICAN ACTOR
(June 28, 1932–November 24, 2005)

Fuck the wax.

Sweep the leg.

Charlie Chaplin

BRITISH ACTOR, FILM DIRECTOR, COMPOSER
(April 16, 1889–December 25, 1977)

· · ·

Jayne Mansfield
Always opt for a hat over a scarf.

Gloria Stuart
Your heart will go on . . . until it doesn't.

Natalie Wood
Life preservers go with everything.

Aaron Spelling
Zip codes matter. Good genes don't.

Ed Wood
Shitty work can still make you famous.

Stanley Kubrick
It's not right until it's perfect. It's not right until it's perfect. It's not right until it's perfect.

James Doohan
CANADIAN ACTOR, VOICEOVER ARTIST
(March 3, 1920–July 20, 2005)

You can only be beamed
up so far.

Albert Einstein

GERMAN-AMERICAN SCIENTIST
(March 14, 1879–April 18, 1955)

E = shampoo, cut, and blow-dry.

Lucille Ball

AMERICAN ACTRESS
(August 6, 1911–April 26, 1989)

In the factory line of life,
sometimes you just have to
stuff your bra.

Lewis Carroll
If there's grass on the field, it's okay to jump
through the looking glass.

Clark Gable
Just don't give a damn.

Michael Crichton
Nothing's dead forever.

Phil Harris
Fishing for crab might be the deadliest job, but a three-packs-a-day habit will kill you first.

J. M. Barrie
Be a little boy forever.
There's nothing wrong with never growing up.

Chris Benoit
What's so bad about a good, ol' fashioned divorce?

Elizabeth Taylor

AMERICAN ACTRESS, PHILANTHROPIST
(February 27, 1932–March 23, 2011)

Marry early.

Marry often.

Audrey Hepburn

BRITISH ACTRESS, HUMANITARIAN
(May 4, 1929–January 20, 1993)

Never be afraid to overdress
for breakfast.

Farrah Fawcett

AMERICAN ACTRESS, ARTIST
(February 2, 1947–June 25, 2009)

When it comes to angels,
blonde is better.

Ted Williams
Everything keeps longer on ice.

Margaret Mitchell
Look both ways before you cross the street . . .
or else you'll be gone with the wind.

Rocky Marciano
Quit while you're ahead.

Charles Darwin
If you're worried about evolution,
don't marry your cousin.

Sigmund Freud
When in doubt, blame your mother.

Martin Luther King
Feed the hungry. Clothe the naked.
Don't stand on an open hotel balcony if you're
pushing for civil rights in the Deep South.

Bea Arthur

AMERICAN ACTRESS, COMEDIAN, SINGER
(May 13, 1922–April 25, 2009)

Always be a giant
amongst women.

Marilyn Monroe

AMERICAN ACTRESS, SINGER, MODEL
(June 1, 1926–August 5, 1962)

Barbiturates
are a girl's best friend.

Judy Garland

AMERICAN ACTRESS, SINGER
(June 10, 1922–June 22, 1969)

Turns out the other side of
the rainbow isn't at the
bottom of a bottle of scotch.

Anna Nicole Smith

AMERICAN ACTRESS, MODEL, TELEVISION PERSONALITY
(November 28, 1967–February 8, 2007)

Money doesn't grow on trees,

but it does come from rich old

guys if you have double Ds.

Jimmy Stewart

AMERICAN ACTOR

(May 20, 1908–July 2, 1997)

It's a wonderful life—

until you're dead.

Caligula
Never stop horsing around.

Jesus
Stop telling people I told you to do stupid shit.

Marie Curie
You might think you look pretty,
but when you start to glow in the dark
it's time for a Silkwood shower.

Julius Caesar

If a psychic tells you to stay home
on the fifteenth of March, do it.

Timothy Leary

Turn on, tune in, drop out,
and get your prostate checked annually.

John Hughes

Life moves pretty fast. If you don't stop and look
around once in a while, you could miss it.

Alfred Hitchcock

BRITISH DIRECTOR, PRODUCER
(August 13, 1899–April 29, 1980)

Make sure they always get
your good side.

John Belushi

AMERICAN COMEDIAN, ACTOR, MUSICIAN
(January 24, 1949–March 5, 1982)

There is nothing more valuable than a higher education.

Chris Farley

AMERICAN COMEDIAN, ACTOR
(February 15, 1964–December 18, 1997)

Emulating Belushi can
only go so far.

Lisa "Left Eye" Lopes
What about your seatbelt?

Jeffrey Dahmer
You are what you eat.

Dave Thomas
Do yourself a favor and try to choke down
a Biggie Salad every once in awhile.

Marvin Gaye

No matter how bad things get,
don't move back in with your folks.

Johnny Cash

A man can only expect to live so long when he's
been dressed for a funeral for his entire life.

Selena

Run background checks before
you hire the new chick.

Rodney Dangerfield

AMERICAN COMEDIAN, ACTOR
(November 22, 1921–October 5, 2004)

I'll tell ya, if you want some respect, put down the bong.

George Carlin

AMERICAN COMEDIAN, ACTOR, AUTHOR
(May 12, 1937–June 22, 2008)

F*#k all those pissed-off,

c*#t-licking, c!*ksucking,

sh*t-eating, tit-shaking

motherf*#kers!

Babe Ruth

AMERICAN BASEBALL PLAYER
(February 6, 1895–August 16, 1948)

Just because they name a candy bar after you doesn't mean it's all you should eat.

André the Giant

FRENCH WRESTLER, ACTOR
(May 19, 1946–January 27, 1993)

Try not to take
nicknames to heart.

Aaliyah
Overcrowding isn't just a problem in China.

Michael Hutchence
Never underestimate the importance
of the buddy system.

John Phillips
A family that plays together, stays together.

Sylvia Plath
Always bake with a preheated oven.

Jim Henson
Contrary to popular belief,
you can catch pneumonia from
sticking your hand up a puppet's ass.

Jim Varney
There's an importance to being Ernest.

Bobby Kennedy

AMERICAN POLITICIAN
(November 20, 1925–June 6, 1968)

Those who forget family history are doomed to repeat it.

John F. Kennedy

AMERICAN PRESIDENT
(May 29, 1917–November 22, 1963)

Don't mess with Texas.

Ronald Reagan

AMERICAN PRESIDENT
(February 6, 1911–June 5, 2004)

Never forget to . . . Wait . . .
I totally forget what I was
about to say . . .

Benjamin Franklin

INVENTOR, AUTHOR, PHILOSOPHER, PRINTER, POLITICAL THEORIST,
FOUNDING FATHER, SATIRIST, AND SCIENTIST
(January 17, 1706–April 17, 1790)

Screw virtue.

Don't be afraid to indulge in

a vice every once in awhile.

Lee Harvey Oswald
Deny, deny, deny.

Jeff Conaway
A hickey from Kenickie is like a Hallmark card.

Emily Brontë
Keep clear of the moors.

John Wilkes Booth
Sometimes breaking a leg isn't the best advice.

Joan of Arc
If God tells you to dress like a boy and try
to save a nation, ask Him how to avoid the
inevitable burning at the stake.

Thomas Jefferson
Don't shit where you eat.

Princess Diana

Princess of Wales
(July 1, 1961–August 31, 1997)

Would it kill you to stop for a picture?

Richard Nixon

AMERICAN PRESIDENT
(January 9, 1913–April 22, 1994)

Always destroy the evidence.

Saddam Hussein

IRAQI PRESIDENT
(April 28, 1937–December 30, 2006)

There's nothing wrong with roughing it . . . as long as you have "The Greatest Love of All" and a bag of Cool Ranch Doritos to keep you company.

Theodore Roosevelt

Speak softly and carry a big stick and then you can give it to your cousin if he can't walk.

Lyndon B. Johnson

Be careful what you wish for.

Jimmy Carter

Buy stock in peanut butter.

Paul Revere
Call ahead.

George Washington
Don't joke around when it comes to dental care.

Amelia Earhart
Don't leave home without a GPS.

Al Capone

AMERICAN GANGSTER

(January 17, 1899–January 25, 1947)

Hire an accountant
you can trust.

Henry VIII

KING OF ENGLAND, KING OF IRELAND, CLAIMANT TO THE KINGDOM OF
FRANCE, SECOND MONARCH TO THE HOUSE OF TUDOR
(June 28, 1491–January 28, 1547)

If at first you don't conceive,
try, try, try, try, try again.

Adolf Hitler

GERMAN DICTATOR, LEADER OF THE
NATIONAL SOCIALIST GERMAN WORKERS PARTY
(April 20, 1889–April 30, 1945)

A good mustache never goes out of style.

Sammy Davis, Jr.

AMERICAN DANCER, SINGER, COMEDIAN, ACTOR
(December 8, 1925–May 16, 1990)

Keep one eye

on the prize.

Boris Karloff

Nothing's wrong with replacement parts.

Jonathan Brandis

Chuck Norris's tears can cure cancer . . .
but they can't save a sidekick's career.

Cary Grant

Sleeping with your coworkers
is completely acceptable.

J. R. R. Tolkien
Chicks dig guys who speak Elvish.

Pedro Zamora
Reality television will be the death of all of us.

Stieg Larsson
If you want to be a famous author,
chick lit is your safest bet.

Mother Teresa

INDIAN HUMANITARIAN, CATHOLIC NUN
(August 26, 1910–September 5, 1997)

Not getting laid doesn't
make you a saint.

Mahatma Gandhi

INDIAN PHILOSOPHER, LEADER, PHILANTHROPIST
(October 2, 1869–January 30, 1948)

Treat yourself to a
hamburger every
once in awhile.

Sid Vicious

BRITISH MUSICIAN
(May 10, 1957–February 2, 1979)

You can always count on
Mum to come through
in the clutch.

Jerry Garcia

AMERICAN MUSICIAN, ARTIST
(August 1, 1942–August 9, 1995)

You know you've made it when they name an ice-cream after you.

Buddy Holly

AMERICAN MUSICIAN
(September 7, 1936–February 3, 1959)

Take the bus.

Jimmy Hoffa
Sometimes you just have to compromise.

Dr. Kevorkian
Dying is not a choice,
but second-degree murder sure is.

Andy Kaufman
Always leave them guessing.

Bob Hope
Everyone's gotta go sometime.

Phil Hartman
Never go to bed angry.

George Steinbrenner
Idiocy is genetic.

Elvis Presley

American Musician, Actor, U.S. Army Private
(January 8, 1935–August 16, 1977)

Just because you're king doesn't mean you have to die on the throne.

The Notorious B.I.G.

AMERICAN RAPPER
(May 21, 1972–March 9, 1997)

Four hundred pounds of
fat does not equal
one bullet-proof vest.

Tupac Shakur

American Rapper
(June 16, 1971–September 13, 1996)

California knows how
to party, but give
New York a shot.

Kurt Cobain

AMERICAN MUSICIAN
(February 20, 1967–April 5, 1994)

It won't smell like teen spirit after you've been in the attic for a few days.

Frank Sinatra

AMERICAN ACTOR, SINGER
(December 15, 1915–May 14, 1998)

Rubbing elbows with undesirables can do wonders for your career.

Christopher Reeve
Even the man of steel is no match for a horse.

John Holmes
Speak softly and carry a big stick.

J. Edgar Hoover
No matter what anyone says,
silk panties are more comfortable than cotton.

Orson Welles
You shouldn't believe everything
you hear on the radio.

Michael Landon
A little house on the prairie is no place for a fairy.

Grace Kelly
A princess should never drive herself anywhere.

Janis Joplin

AMERICAN SINGER

(January 19, 1943–October 4, 1970)

Not all clubs are cool to join.

Michael Jackson

AMERICAN MUSICIAN, DANCER, ACTOR
(August 29, 1958–June 25, 2009)

When hosting guests over-
night, it's your responsibility
to make sure they're given
comfortable accommodations.

Osama bin Laden
Sometimes SEALS club back.

Patrick Swayze
Nobody puts cancer in the corner.

Leslie Nielsen
Surely, you mustn't take death so seriously.

Dennis Hopper
Life's not an easy ride—
that's where the drugs come in.

James Cagney
Even the top of the world is
filled with no good dirty rats.

John Wayne
Bad habits are hard to break, pilgrim.

Jim Morrison

AMERICAN MUSICIAN
(December 8, 1943–July 3, 1971)

Baths can be nice every

once in awhile,

but watch how much time

you spend in there.

Bob Marley

JAMAICAN MUSICIAN
(February 6, 1945–May 11, 1981)

Don't forget your sunscreen.

Jimi Hendrix

AMERICAN MUSICIAN
(November 27, 1942–September 18, 1970)

Sleep on your side.

Freddie Mercury

BRITISH MUSICIAN
(September 5, 1946–November 24, 1991)

Real champions

wear condoms.

Layne Staley

Kick the smack or you'll really end
up the "man in the box."

Gene Kelly

Remember to bring an umbrella
if you plan on singin' in the rain.

Paul Newman

An organic vinaigrette is the perfect
compliment to any summer salad.

Anthony Perkins

A boy's best friend is his mother.

DeForest Kelley

Dammit man, become a doctor!

Roy Scheider

Buy the bigger boat.

James Brown

AMERICAN MUSICIAN

(May 3, 1933–December 25, 2006)

Even a nickname as cool as "The Godfather of Soul" can only keep you feeling so good (so good).

Sonny Bono

AMERICAN MUSICIAN, POLITICIAN, ACTOR
(February 16, 1935–January 5, 1998)

When a Kennedy offers you
ski lessons, politely decline.

George Harrison

BRITISH MUSICIAN
(February 25, 1943–November 29, 2001)

Keep an eye on the Slow Hand that's trying to steal the Hot Wife.

Steve Irwin

AUSTRALIAN ANIMAL RIGHTS ACTIVIST, TV PERSONALITY
(February 22, 1962–September 4, 2006)

Sometimes a little barb

can go too far.

Edward Kennedy
Swimming lessons are worth every penny.

Karl Marx
Share and share alike.

Anne Boleyn
Never lose your head over a married man.

Randy "Macho Man" Savage
Snap into a Slim Jim.

Leonardo da Vinci
A code was meant to be broken . . . but you'll still never know why she's smiling.

Anne Frank
You can run, but you can't hide.

Mr. Rogers

AMERICAN TELEVISION PERSONALITY
(March 20, 1928–February 27, 2003)

Cardigans go with everything, Neighbor.

Vincent Price

AMERICAN ACTOR
(May 27, 1911–October 25, 1993)

No matter how cool it seems at the time, no one wants to be remembered as the creepy guy.

Heath Ledger

AUSTRALIAN ACTOR
(April 4, 1979–January 22, 2008)

Be selective when choosing
your emergency contact.

Bob Ross

AMERICAN PAINTER, ART INSTRUCTOR, TELEVISION PERSONALITY
(October 29, 1942–July 4, 1995)

Never paint yourself into
a corner without painting
a happy little door to exit
through.

Edgar Allan Poe

AMERICAN AUTHOR, POET, LITERARY CRITIC
(January 19, 1809–October 7, 1849)

Absinthe makes the heart grow fonder.

Brittany Murphy
You must be *Clueless* to mix that many pills.

Linda Lovelace
Train yourself not to gag—
it might make you famous one day.

Vivien Leigh
The kindness of strangers won't
keep the plantation running.

Eartha Kitt

That whole nine lives thing
doesn't apply to Catwoman.

Zelda Rubinstein

Don't go toward the light.

Bettie Page

A pin up a day keeps the debt collectors at bay.

Johnny Carson

AMERICAN COMEDIAN, TELEVISION PERSONALITY
(October 23, 1925–January 23, 2005)

Carnac says

the answer is . . .

Ed McMahon

AMERICAN COMEDIAN, TV PERSONALITY, VOICEOVER ARTIST
(March 6, 1923–June 23, 2009)

Being a sidekick is a lot of laughs, but it won't pay your bills.

Walt Disney

AMERICAN PRODUCER, DIRECTOR, SCREENWRITER,
ANIMATOR, ENTREPRENEUR
(December 5, 1901–December 15, 1966)

If you build it,

overcharge.

Billy Mays

American Salesperson
(July 20, 1958–June 28, 2009)

BILLY MAYS HERE TO TELL YOU THAT TOO MUCH YELLING CAN CAUSE A HEART ATTACK!

Rod Serling

AMERICAN SCREENWRITER, NOVELIST, VOICEOVER ARTIST
(December 25, 1924–June 28, 1975)

Always check the airplane
wing for stowaways.

Ryan Dunn
It's better to burn out than to fade away.

Elizabeth Edwards
It's never too late to separate.

Abraham Lincoln
Box seats are for bitches.

Joe DiMaggio
Don't be fooled;
blondes really aren't more fun.

Gianni Versace
A PO box, while sometimes inconvenient,
is a relatively safe way to receive your mail.

Margaret Hamilton
Every girl needs a good pair of shoes.

William Shakespeare

BRITISH POET, PLAYWRIGHT
(April 26, 1564–April 23, 1616)

Departing

is such sweet sorrow.

DAILY BENDER

Want Some More?

Hit up our humor blog, The Daily Bender, to get your fill of all things funny—be it subversive, odd, offbeat, or just plain mean. The Bender editors are there to get you through the day and on your way to happy hour. Whether we're linking to the latest video that made us laugh or calling out (or bullshit on) whatever's happening, we've got what you need for a good laugh.

If you like our book, you'll love our blog. (And if you hated it, "man up" and tell us why.) Visit The Daily Bender for a shot of humor that'll serve you until the bartender can.

Sign up for our newsletter at
www.adamsmedia.com/blog/humor
and download our Top Ten Maxims No Man Should Live Without.